SEEING ROME
& CHRISTIAN ITALY

*A Guide to What
Evangelicals Usually Miss*

Royal L. Peck

RECLAIMED
PUBLISHING

RECLAIMED PUBLISHING

Seeing Rome and Christian Italy: A Guide to What Evangelicals Usually Miss
Copyright © 2012 Royal L. Peck
All rights reserved.
Published by Reclaimed Publishing
             a publishing division of Reclaimed, Inc.
             22030 NE 73rd St.
             Redmond, WA 98053

Cover design: John Mark Warkentin
Front Cover photo: Didier Baertschiger

First printing 2012

Printed in the United States of America

ISBN 13: 978-0615636153
ISBN 10: 0615636152

CONTENTS

Foreword

I spent my eighth birthday in Rome. It was 1988 and my grandparents had been in Italy for thirty-three years. Despite a bad first impression in 1952 which led my grandpa to declare Italy to be "the armpit of Europe," God moved my grandparents to respond to the need for a Bible school in Rome. They packed up their three small children and their belongings to make a home in a land which felt a world away.

For nearly two decades of my life, I received packages every month, each one covered in Italian stamps. They held letters, newspaper clippings on European fashion, and Italian panties. Since Grandma was the one to shop for these pretty things, Grandpa decided to enclose crisp American dollar bills – where did he get those in Italy? – to get some credit for these special arrivals too. In a way, I grew up with reminders of Italy every thirty-one days.

By the time of my first trip, Grandpa had become a living encyclopedia on Italy. A walk through grand churches or a tour of the Coliseum became a stroll through history. Grandpa told detailed stories about the faithful Christians who had gone before us. Our Christian heritage came alive. I could ask him anything from what happened in the book of Acts to the influences of the Renaissance and he knew about it! He saw Italy. He and Grandma had become fluent, not just in a new language, but in all things Italian.

We visited *miei nonni* on several other occasions and every time my love for Italy grew. My grandfather has finally written down the histories which fascinated me as child (and as an adult). They are pieces of God's story as it unfolded in Italy. It is with great joy that I recommend this book to you as you begin to see Christian Italy for yourself.

Andiamo,

Renée Rinehart
California
May 2012

Introduction

Seeing Italy should be of utmost importance for any tourist. An ancient Italian proverb declares: "Vedi Napoli e poi muori." This play on words: "See Naples and die," to the Neopolitan means "Having seen the beauty of Naples one needs to see nothing more before dying." This is how I feel about all of Italy. Villages with thousand year old buildings dot mountaintops from north to south. Medieval cities like Venice and Florence point back to the Renaissance. The art of Michelangelo, Raphael, and Giotto permeate city after city. And then there's Rome, *la città eterna*. No other nation is so rich in history, art, and culture.

But in addition to Italy's "must see" sites and cities, it is also a land rich in archeological and biblical remains. Most of these places are little known. Few Italian guides are aware of what evangelicals need to see. Even fewer know where to find these places. If the evangelical tourist leaves Italy without seeing and understanding the Bible and Reformation sites of this formidable land, he or she has missed much of what Italy has to offer.

After my wife and I founded the Italian Bible Institute in 1958, friends began to ask us to help them see the Italy that evangelicals usually miss. Commercial tours just weren't taking people to many important sites. It was then that we began our serious research. We talked to people, read books, and tracked our own travel experiences. We shared this material for many years as we escorted friends and Christian groups around Italy. At one point we even had our own tour company in Rome.

Our fifty-seven years as missionaries in Italy has given us a love for Christian history and for Christianity's impact upon Italy. Now at last we can make this content available to more of God's people.

This book is outlined into travel itineraries. We begin where the Apostle Paul began and follow him all the way into Rome. Feel free to dip into sections that accompany your own travels or skip ahead to the places that interest you most. In the end, our prayer is that this book will not only open your eyes to enjoy Italy as never before, but also enrich your life as a Christian.

Cheerily yours,

Royal & Elizabeth Peck

Southern Italy

Syracuse

No one really knows when the Christian church began in Italy. Perhaps a Jew from Rome was one of the 5,000 men converted to Jesus Christ on the day of Pentecost (Acts 2:5-10; 4:4). Maybe he carried the gospel from Jerusalem back to Italy. On the other hand, it could have been the Italian Centurion Cornelius, converted under Peter's ministry in Caesarea, who took the Good News to Rome. However it happened, we know that by the time the Apostle Paul reached Italy there were already thriving communities of Christians throughout the peninsula.

The Bible records Paul's arrival in Italy in Acts 28:11-16. It reads like a travel log:

> "After three months we set sail in a ship that had wintered in the island, a ship of Alexandria, with the twin gods as a figurehead. Putting in at Syracuse, we stayed there for three days. And from there we made a circuit and arrived at Rhegium. And after one day a

south wind sprang up, and on the second day we
came to Puteoli. There we found brothers and were
invited to stay with them for seven days. And so we
came to Rome. And the brothers there, when they
heard about us, came as far as the Forum of Appius
and Three Taverns to meet us. On seeing them, Paul
thanked God and took courage. And when we came
into Rome, Paul was allowed to stay by himself, with
the soldier that guarded him."

Visiting Syracuse

After sailing from the island of Malta Paul's ship stopped at the
Sicilian port of Syracuse (*Siracusa*). Acts 28:12 records, "putting
in at Syracuse, we stayed there for three days." Syracuse's natural
harbor made it one of the Mediterranean's major ports. The
Apostle Paul had three days on his hands in a city famous in the
ancient world.

Cicero lauded the beauty of Syracuse saying: "...it is the most
beautiful of all the Greek cities...it doesn't know a day the sun
does not shine." Archemides, one of the ancient world's greatest
scientists, was born and labored here. Iceta of Syracuse (who
discovered the rotation of the earth 2,000 years before Galileo)
was also born here. Plato relates that he was forty years old when
he visited Syracuse for the first time. He disliked the life-style he
found there and lamented: "The Syracusans and the Italiotti

(Italians) call "happy" their habit of daily banquets at which they gorge themselves twice a day, never passing a night without someone in bed with them, and pursuing everything that makes these occupations possible."

Perhaps Paul was able to see some of the city's magnificent monuments. A **16,000 seat Greek Amphitheater** hosted Greek theater dramas. Fifth-century BC inscriptions of the names of various gods can still be seen on the walls of the corridors.

Also nearby is the **Archaeological Park of the Neapolis**, home to the **Latomia of Paradise**, a series of twelve grotto-caves with towering natural walls. Here in 413 BC. thousands of Athenian prisoners were held captive after the Siracusans rebelled against Athenian occupation. All but a few of the prisoners died here.

From beside the Amphitheater you have a great view of the entirety of L'Orecchio di Dinosio. Literally, Ear of Dionysus, this well-known cave has marvelous acoustics—try singing yourself to enjoy its merit! Continuing eastward, have a look inside the most spectacular of all the caves, Latomia dei Cappuccini.

Perhaps, the apostle was able to engage with people as he did in Athens and found out about **the sacrifice altar of the tyrant Gerone II**. This altar was the largest known to the Greek world (198 meters long and 22,80 meters wide) and according to the historian Diodoro Siculo (80-20 BC circa) four hundred and fifty oxen were sacrificed in one day to the god Jove, the Liberator.

The oldest section of the city, the lanes of the **Isle of Ortigia**, is a great architectural walk for admiring numerous Palazzi (palaces) of Siracusan nobility.

Aretusa Fountain: this famous, fresh water spring was renowned in antiquity by Pindar and Virgil. Today it continues to gush plentifully into a picturesque basin planted with papyri.

Syracuse is the only area of Italy where Papyrus is grown. The **Papyrus Museum** contains ancient papyruses dating back to the fifteenth century BC.

Finally, the beautiful **port area** is a great place to imagine what it must have been like for Paul to arrive here. Although, Paul and Luke appear not to have been aware of any believers in Syracuse, by the end of the first century, Syracuse had a fervent body of Christ that was second only to the church in Antioch. The Church in Antioch sent to Syracuse one of their best evangelists, Marcian. He had been discipled by the Apostle Peter. In short order he led many converts to Christ. His zeal and efficacy turned the pagan community against him. According to tradition he was martyred before the second century began.

Reggio di Calabria

Paul's second stop on his way from Malta to Rome is mentioned in Acts with only eleven words: "And from there we made a circuit and arrived at Rhegium." (Acts 28:13) His ship stopped at this port on the tip of the boot of the Italian peninsula for one day.

Rhegium *(Reggio di Calabria)* is on the mainland of Italy, just before reaching the Straits of Messina. The Straits separate the Island of Sicily from the mainland of Italy by only 3 kilometers and are a treacherous stretch of water.

The Christian roots of Reggio are unknown, but it is clear that the city was evangelized very early. The first mention of a Christian Bishop occurs when Mark, Bishop of Rhegium, is mentioned as being a legate at the Council of Nicea (325 AD). Jerome (340-420 AD) in his letter 146 *To Evangelus* indicates there is a Bishop in Rhegium. However, it was captured and destroyed by Dionysius, tyrant of Syracuse, in 387 BC, when all the surviving inhabitants were sold into slavery (Diodorus xiv. 106-8, 111, 112)

In the fourth century a vibrant community of Jews established itself in Reggio. The Jews were very active for nearly twelve hundred years. It was in Reggio that the first dated Hebrew book was published in 1475—Rashi's commentary on the Pentateuch, the most famous exegesis of the Jewish Pentatuch. Rashi is still regarded by Jewish theologians as one of Israel's most influential scholars of biblical exegesis. His work influenced some Christian thinkers as early as the twelfth century.

However, in 1492 not only did King Ferdinand II of Aragon and his wife Isabella commission Christopher Columbus to explore the ends of the Atlantic Ocean, but also they forcefully drove the Jews from their kingdom. They inaugurated the Spanish Inquisition throughout their reign of Spain, Sicily and Naples. Yet, within a generation Martin Luther would nail his ninety-five theses to a church door in Wittenberg and begin the Protestant Reformation.

Visiting Reggio di Calabria

Today, the fifteenth century **castle built for King Ferdinand II of Aragon** can still be seen. Also, **Via Giudecca** is where the Jewish community was located prior to being expelled in 1492. Lastly, walk the ocean-front street **Lungomare** to see the ancient walls of the Greek city and the Roman Baths.

Guardia Piemontese

On Paul's journey northwest from Reggio to Puteoli his ship passed within view of a mountain. On it a Protestant village of refuge would be built. It would be the home of many thousands of Waldensians Christians who moved from the restricted confines of the Waldensian valleys near Turin in northern Italy. On this mountain-top these godly precursors of Martin Luther would find peace and protection for over two hundred years. Sadly, the peace of this refuge ended in a bloody massacre.

Waldensian History

As the Roman empire declined and finally fell, Latin began to disappear as the language of government. By the second half of the sixth century it had disappeared altogether. In the West, Greek was known only by the nobility and the educated. In the Byzantine East, *Koiné* Greek was the basis of a literary language and gained ascendancy in official usage as well. As the breach between the literate and illiterate grew wider and wider, the Bible became the unique domain of the clergy. The common people's knowledge of God depended mostly on the official church leaders, but the spiritual life of these religious professionals declined, deepening the darkness for the masses.

Peter Waldo

In the year 1170, God saved a rich merchant in Lyon, France and moved him to do something about the spiritual plight that affected the people in his city. Following a deep spiritual experience, Peter Waldo gave all his possessions to the poor and needy and began to fearlessly preach the gospel in public squares throughout Lyon. Hundreds gave their lives to Christ and experienced the same radical change as Waldo had. In turn they began to preach freely in the open air and gave personal testimony to what God had done in their lives. They identified themselves as the "Poor Men of Lyon" (i.e. poor in spirit) and regarded themselves as a church within the Church, a select circle who sought to revive the church.

Authorities of the Roman Catholic diocese ordered Waldo and his followers to cease their preaching. Preaching the gospel was seen as the mission of the clergy and only successors of the apostles (Priests, Bishops, Monks etc.) had the authority to preach. The "Poor Men of Lyon", now known as Waldensians, were forcefully excommunicated in 1184 by the Council of

Verona. Waldo's followers spread throughout Savoy (Southern France and Northern Italy). The narrow alpine valleys located in the Turin area offered a secure haven. Having disposed of their own private property, they offered themselves as peasants on the farms of the wealthy and noble. Although their rapid growth of converts slowed, the Waldensians succeeded at preserving their faith in Christ and the Scriptures.

Waldensians Migrate to Calabria

By the fourteenth century the Waldensian population had outgrown the northern valleys. Fewer farms needed additional peasant help in the relative safe valleys of the North. Young families felt forced to offer themselves as share-croppers elsewhere. It was at this time Zanino del Poggio, a wealthy landowner, from Calabria visited the northern alpine valleys and offered the Waldensians the rich land in Calabria.

Many made the move and established a new community near the existing village of Montalto Uffugo a few kilometers NW of Cosenza. Within a few years Waldensian communities lived in peace with their neighbors and privately practiced their faith in Guardia, San Sisto, San Vincenzo la Costa, and Vaccarizzo.

In 1557 traveling evangelists from the northern valleys urged their Calabrian brothers to join the reformation movements of Germany and Switzerland. Public worship services began and the Waldensian temple in Guardia was built.

Inquisition Begins

Open practice of their faith upset Cardinal Ghislieri (who later became Pius V). The mountain-top village of Guardia seemed secure behind its walls, but the night of June 5, 1561 proved otherwise.

Under pressure from the Cardinal, Marquis Spinelli of Fuscaldo dressed his small army of fifty soldiers in chains and the garb of prisoners. In the wee hours of the morning he sent them to the city gates, Guardia Piemontese. The guards were told that Marquis Spinelli had ordered these prisoners to be kept in Guardia until morning when they would be transferred to the prison in Fuscaldo. The guards opened the gates.

Once inside the walls, the false prisoners shed their garments and began to use their hidden weapons to order each head of house to reconvert to Catholicism. All who refused were killed on the spot. In the next few days 2,000 Waldensians were massacred. According to survivors the streets of Guardia ran with rivers of blood, reaching the main gate of the city. Hence the name: The Gate of Blood (Porta del Sangue).

The Waldensians who renounced their faith were sentenced to seven severe penalties lasting for twenty-five years:

1. Marriage between two Waldensians was forbidden.
2. No more than six Waldensians could meet together for any gathering inside or outside.

3. Men had to wear the "sanbenito" (a yellow cape with a large red cross on the front.)

4. All had to attend mass every day at the local Catholic Church.

5. Women could no longer wear the traditional costume of the area, but were forced to wear a unique head covering called a "penaglio".

6. They were forbidden to speak to one another in their native language "Occitana". (This language continues to be spoken in Guardia and is not understood by other residents in Calabria or elsewhere in Italy.)

7. The front door to every house had to have a "peep door" that could be opened only from the outside. This "spy door" was used daily by Jesuit priests who went throughout the village spying to make certain the people were saying the rosary at the appointed hour.

Visiting Guardia Piemontese

Brilliant views of the Mediterranean await from this quiet village. A two hour walking tour will bring to life the stories of the past. Follow the city walls to find the Porta del Sangue. Also, see if you can find the monument placed where the Waldensian Temple once stood. Elderly locals may offer themselves as guides, though few speak English. Ask to see the museum, which is opened only upon request and be sure to leave a small tip for your guide.

Today most inhabitants of the village are non-religious and agnostic in faith. Those who know the history of their village give no thought as to its significance. Although there is a local Roman Catholic Church, few take communion. Those we spoke with did not know of any evangelicals who live in Guardia Piemontese.

Pozzuoli, Pompeii and Naples

Acts 28:13-14, "And after one day a south wind sprang up, and on the second day we came to Puteoli. There we found brothers and were invited to stay with them for seven days. And so we came to Rome."

Paul's voyage to Rome neared its end. Six or seven months have passed since Paul left Caesarea and his "brig-days" were over. Rome, Nero and the beginning of his trial were just a few short kilometers to the northwest. But first, he and his companion Luke, his jailor, and the other prisoners disembarked amid the hubbub of Rome's major port of entry. Grain and other agricultural goods would have been loaded and unloaded from the numerous ships all around them. Fishermen must have loudly hawked their fresh catch of the day. Merchants bought, sold, and bartered.

Puetoli (*now called Pozzuoli*) and Pompeii were both thriving port cities in Paul's day. Naples, known as *Neapolis* to the ancients, also flourished, sponsoring Olympic style games called Sebasta every five years. Many of the Italian peninsula's most beautiful cities are still found in the Naples area.

Although Pozzuoli (Puteoli) is no longer one of Italy's major ports, the early morning hours somewhat resemble the commotion that was going on 2,000 years ago. The covered fish market building is great to visit early on a weekday morning. Amidst the fish merchants the sights, sounds, and smells will easily carry you back to the first-century experience of Paul and Luke.

Visiting Pozzuoli

Many rich and famous ancient Romans had villas in Puteoli (*Pozzuoli*). One of them was Cicero (106-43 BC), who called Puteoli "Little Rome". Romans considered the mineral springs that bubble up from the Solfatara volcano beneath the city to be efficacious for the cure of various diseases. Virgil (70-19 BC), author of the famous epic *Aeneid* is buried in Puteoli. Additionally, Horace (65 BC-8 BC), expressed his love of the oysters and mussels cultivated in Puteoli.

In spite of its ancient fame, Pozzuoli was largely ignored until the 1950's when aerial photographs and underwater investigation by Italian military pilot Raimondo Bucher brought Pozzuoli to modern-day fame. Excavation that began in 1991 has revealed that the ruins of Puteoli are in no way inferior to what is to be seen in Pompeii and Herculeum.

Pliny the Elder (23–79 AD) described **Pozzuoli's port** as one of the most magnificent and marvelous works of antiquity. More than a mile and a half of ancient Puteoli is submerged along the shores of present Pozzuoli and the remains of **Portus Julius** can be seen by glass-bottom boat or guided sub-tours. Picture the water-front where the Apostle Paul and Luke disembarked. Walk through a few of the narrow back streets near the Port to get a flavor of life in this city.

Excavation in the **Rioni Terra** section of the city revealed the street network of the 194 BC city. This underground archaeological route is right in the heart of modern Pozzuoli. See a system of small, narrow cells used for the slaves, **Ergastula**, below the bakery (pistrinum) along the route of the decumanus. On the walls of one of the widest rooms are two gladiators sketched in charcoal and two verses, probably of a poem.

Plan at least half a day to visit the city on foot. Starting from San Gennaro's Sanctuary walk down Via S. Gennaro Agnano for 300m to reach the **Solfatara volcano**. Follow Via Solfatara for 1km to the **Flavian Amphitheatre** (entrance on Via Terracciano). The amphitheater is the third largest in Italy (381 by 489 feet) and is one of the best preserved. It was begun by Nero and finished shortly after Emperor Vespasian completed the Coliseum in Rome. It seated 20,000 spectators. The subterranean structures are in a perfect state of preservation and nowhere else is it possible to get so clear an idea of the complicated mechanism required for hoisting caged wild beasts up to the arena.

Not far from the Amphitheatre you can see the ruins of an imposing thermal building known as the **Temple of Neptune**. An imposing structure reveals the first century bathing facility. From there you can head for the big intersection of piazza Capomazza and turn right on Villa Celle to see the **Roman Necropolis**, the site of historical tombs and mausoleums dating from 50-100 AD.

Returning to Piazza Capomazza junction and turning left down to Via Pergolesi, after walking past the bridge on the Cumana Railway you reach the **Temple of Setrapis**. Identified for many years as a temple, it is, instead, the remains of the main market place of ancient Puteoli known as the "Macellum". The three columns bear evidence of bradyseism that has placed most of the ancient port area under water. Sixteen columns supported the roof that enclosed the area. You can see the remains of two large rooms which were ancient public lavatories.

Additionally, **Monte Nuovo** was formed by a tremendous volcanic explosion in 1538 and **Lake Avernus** is of volcanic origin and was believed to be the entrance to Hades (the Underworld). On the eastern shore of the lake are the imposing remains of a Bath house long referred to as **Temple of Apollo**, dating back to Hadrian's reign in the second century. Originally, it had a domed roof just a bit smaller than that of the Pantheon in Rome.

Archaeological research continues to unearth important remains of this city of New Testament times. Pozzuoli is becoming one of the most important archaeological parks of Italy and Europe.

Visiting Pompeii

Paul sailed into the bay of Naples a few short years before that fatal August 23, 79 when volcanic Mount Vesuvius exploded with atomic force and buried the thriving cities of Pompeii and Herculeum in its ash and molten lava. Pliny the Younger was in the Bay of Naples and actually saw the eruption as an eyewitness.

In the early 1700s the existence of Pompeii and Herculeum was unknown, though marble artifacts abounded everywhere. These were carried off to decorate the luxurious homes of the Neapolitan rich and many others throughout Europe. A history of looting continued throughout the first half of the 1700s. Scientific investigation of the area began only after this period of looting. What has been preserved of Vesuvius are two entire cities of the Pauline era: Pompei and Herculeum.

Pompeii has preserved a snapshot of the religious culture of the people of that day. Striking murals and mosaics are to be seen throughout the city. It is evident that Pompeii was a luxurious city that provided wealthy residents of Rome with a place for a holiday villa. It was also an international city and had many foreign residents.

The mystery cults of Demeter, Dionysus, and Isis abounded. The temples of Apollo and Jupiter dominated the city's skyline. The followers of Isis, a female goddess from Egypt, erected a small temple in her honor. She offered the worshipper personal salvation. This personal relationship with deity was a new concept to the Italians of that day.

The feminine deity attracted admirers and followers, especially women, many centuries prior to the coming of Christ. The Egyptians called her Isis; the Babilonians, Tiamat; the Greeks, Hera; and the Romans, Jove. Terracotta idols of this goddess have been unearthed at many archaeological sites around the Mediterranean basin. Some of these idols depict a crowned woman sitting on a throne holding a baby in her arms. One of her titles was "Queen of Heaven".

Christianity in Pompeii

Whether there were Christians in Pompeii is uncertain. Graffiti found in Pompeii has been used to support a Christian presence. One of the most discussed graffiti is a drawing of a crucified donkey. It has been interpreted as a parody of the crucifixion of Christ. Persecution experienced under Nero in 64 AD was violent, but short lived. Nevertheless a Christian community in Pompeii would have to be discreet and basically anonymous.

Visiting Naples

Naples, Italy's third largest city, has influenced the culture of Italy from its earliest times. It has rich traditions in history, art, culture, and of course, cuisine. Naples's buildings, museums and language all bear traces of its history. Neapolitan is a colorful, rich Italian dialect known in Naples as *Napulitano*.

Naples, unlike many historical Italian cities, is not a sightseeing town. But if you take the time to explore the local streets in *Centro Storico* (the historical center of Naples), then this ancient Greek town, inhabited continually for three thousand years by the same people, will teach you much. You will discover touches of Italian life and culture, which cannot be found anywhere else in Italy. "Vedi Napoli e poi Muori" ("See Naples and die") is as valid today as it was during the reign of the Bourbons of Naples when the phrase was invented.

Italy's first tomatoes came from America to Naples in the early 1500's and quickly became a staple in the Italian diet. **Pizza** was born in Naples. A classic is Pizza Margherita (simple pizza dough covered with tomato sauce, mozzarella cheese and basil). Neopolitans are so serious about their pizza that a certification board issues recognition to pizza places around the world that are deemed to be making true Neapolitan pizza. One of the requirements? A wood-burning brick oven!

Melanzane alla parmigiana, fried slices of eggplant gratinéed and layered with tomato sauce and parmesan cheese, also originated in Naples. Neapolitan gelato also rates as some of the best ice cream in the world.

A world-class museum well worth visiting is the **National Archeological Museum**. It is best to visit this museum before going to Pompeii. If you go, you must see: Hercules, the Farnese Bull, mosaics and art from Pompeii, Herculeum and the Baths of Caracalla in Rome; see especially the huge battle scene with Alexander the Great.

The **Catacombs of St. Janarius (San Gennaro)** and **The Duomo (Cathedral)** both have claimed the bones of St. Janarius at different times. Now the relics of St. Janarius, including his skull, are kept here in the Chapel of St. Janarius' Treasury.

Purgatorio dell'arca (located in via dei Tribunali 39) is a church that has been the place for devotees to the Cult of Purgative Souls (the wandering souls in Purgatory) since the 1700s. It contains thousands of skulls and bones that are dearly worshipped, despite the fact the cult was banned by the Cardinal of Naples in 1969.

In 716 AD, when Christians in the eastern half of Christendom rejected image and relic worship, most monks refused to abandon their devotion to pictures, statues and relics. Because of the resulting iconoclast persecution hundreds fled to Italy. (Iconoclasm in Greek means "Image-breaking"). Many were given refuge in **San Gregorio Armeno Church** and its monastic complex. The existing monastery was built in 1572 and is now inhabited by Nuns.

Christianity in Naples

Christianity flourished in Naples very early. Catacombs found in the Naples area indicate there was a Christian community by the early second century. In 395 AD Theodosius divided the Roman Empire into the Western and Eastern Empires, with Milan and Constantinople as their capitals. The gradual process of estrangement between the churches of the East and West began at this time. It culminated in the schism between the churches of the East and the West in 1054. Although Southern Italy was aligned with the Roman church, it was greatly influenced by Greek Christianity.

Orthodox rites were commonly held in and around Naples. There was even a Greek monastery in use here until the Counter-Reformation in the seventeenth century. Visitors to the Duomo (Cathedral) will still find a double baptistery inside, one for Roman Catholic rites (sprinkling) and the other for Greek rites (immersion). No one can explain how it began, but a benediction by a Greek Orthodox priest is considered particularly useful by otherwise quite Roman Catholic Neapolitans. It is, according to their superstition, one of the ways in which the so-called malocchio, the 'evil eye,' can be warded off. Many Neapolitans live under the fear of occult evil and consult witches and saints to escape their enemies' wicked incantations.

Neapolitans have more interest in spiritual matters than do most northern Italians. For a fact, evangelistic efforts by Protestant-evangelicals of all denominations have been very fruitful in southern Italy and there are many churches. Some of Italy's largest Evangelical churches are located in this region. Poverty caused many Southerners to emigrate north after World War II. For this reason, many Evangelical churches in Northern Italy have been founded by Christians from the south. Sadly, few of these churches have been able to penetrate the culture of the north and remain "Meridionali" (southern) both in number and culture.

The Road to Rome

Paul and Luke left the warmth of fellowship with their brothers and sisters in Puteoli. The chains that bound Paul to his Roman Jailor felt heavier and heavier. The reality of what he would soon face set in. Rome, the control center of the world, was just over the horizon.

> Acts 28:15-16, "And the brothers there, when they heard about us, came as far as the Forum of Appius and Three Taverns to meet us. On seeing them, Paul thanked God and took courage. And when we came into Rome, Paul was allowed to stay by himself, with the soldier that guarded him."

These first-century travelers headed north from Pozzuoli (*Puetoli)* on a road that cut straight through the mountains called Montagna Spaccata (Split Mountain). After 55km they reached

Capua where they joined **the Appian Way**. This "Queen of Roads" build in 312 BC is the oldest and most famous of Roman roads. Built similarly to present-day freeways, it connected the major cities of the south. On it Rome was able rush its armies to far-flung regions of conquest and battle.

The foundation was of heavy stone blocks cemented together with mortar. Over these were laid polygonal blocks of lava that were smoothly and expertly fitted together. Ancient historians indicate that the surface of the road was so smooth it was difficult to see where one block of stone joined the other. The road averaged 20 feet in width and extended south from Rome for 373 Roman miles to Brindisi (a Roman mile equaled 1.5 km or 1.07 US miles). As the main road to Greece, it was built so well that it was used by travelers for centuries. A good day's walk was 27.5 Roman miles or 42 km!

Today, many miles are still intact. On the outskirts of Rome at *Via Appia Antica* you can observe the deep ruts worn in the stone by the chariot wheels and ox carts. Take time to walk along these same ancient stones that the Apostle Paul crossed.

By car you can follow the route of the Appian Way on a modern road called Strada Statale 7 (SS #7). Starting at Capua, this route will take you through the towns of Itri, Fondi, and Terracina on your way into Rome.

Spartacus Trained in Capua

Until just a few decades before Paul passed through Capua, this city had been a major center of the Roman Empire and one of its largest cities. Spartacus trained in Capua at the gladiatorial school of Batiatus before he gathered an army of 120,000 slaves in 73 BC and led a revolt. He and his followers set out to march to freedom over the Alps into Gaul, but the march was defeated in southern Italy by Crassus. Spartacus was killed and 6,000 of his men were crucified along the Appian Way from Capua to Rome (approximately 120 miles). Every 10 yards a cross was erected on each side of the road. The body of the crucified slave was left on the cross to be consumed by birds and animals. The Romans did this as a warning to other slaves. As you drive Capua to Rome, imagine what this would have been like to see.

Paul's journey northward to Rome would have taken him past the city of Capua's huge and famous **amphitheater**. Historians date its construction to the sometime in thirty years before the birth of Jesus. Cicero writes that it seated 100,000 spectators, but modern archaeologists have reduced that figure to 50,000.

As a Roman citizen, Paul would have been aware of what a Roman amphitheater meant. He wrote to the Corinthian Christians, "For I think that God has exhibited us apostles as last of all, like men sentenced to death, because we have become a spectacle to the world." (1Cor. 4:9) As with every other Roman arena, the amphitheater was the scene of bloody gladiator battles.

Spectators came to see killing performed before their very eyes. Now Paul was a part of the procession. Only God knew whether or not he would end up in the center of some arena as part of the bloody program arranged to satisfy the howling crowds.

Visiting Capua

In addition to seeing the second largest Roman **amphitheater**, the **Campano Provincial Museum** hosts an interesting collection of votive statues placed by women in one of the Temples of Capua The Capuan Mothers, dating 600 BC, offered statues to the deity in hopes they would get pregnant and have a healthy child.

Also, ask a ticket seller at the amphitheater to take you to **The Mithraeum** if you're interested to see a subterranean temple devoted to the pagan god Mithras. He was a deity of truth and light worshipped by many in the army in the third century.

Ten miles north of Capua is a well-preserved medieval Christian basilica (925 AD) called **Sant'Angelo in Formis**. It was built on the ruins of a large temple dedicated to Diana.

Rome

Paul & Nero

Without a doubt Rome offers the greatest tourist attractions in Europe, if not in the world. No other city displays such a gamut of historical and artistic sites covering so many centuries of world civilization. We'll begin by recounting Paul's arrival in "the Eternal City."

The gospel had not only spread throughout the Roman Empire, but it had also deeply impacted the empire's heart, the very city that controlled the world. In Rome a vibrant band of God's people spread the good news that Jesus is both Savior and King of Kings. Even the Caesars who proclaimed themselves to be gods were nothing compared to Jesus, the living God. Christians in Rome possessed a faith in Christ so great, so effective, that the reports of what God was doing through them spread to churches everywhere. In Paul's letter to Rome, he wrote,

"I thank my God through Jesus Christ for all of you,
because your faith is proclaimed in all the world...I
want you to know, brothers, that I have often
intended to come to you (but thus far have been
prevented), in order that I may reap some harvest
among you as well as among the rest of the
Gentiles...So I am eager to preach the gospel to you
also who are in Rome.

(Romans 1:8, 13, 15)

Paul longed to see for himself what was happening in the
world's greatest city and to preach the gospel there. Now he had
arrived, though not as he might have expected.

"The brothers" who originally met Paul on the Appian Way
at the Forum of Apias (present day Borgo Faiti) walked 64 km,
for that greeting. The others met him 20 km closer at Three
Taverns (present day Cisterna). The small band of Christians
walked and talked with Paul for the next thirty-six hours on that
road that led to Rome. Through the Alban Hills and past the
villages of Velletri and Albano they walked, until at last they saw
the city's imposing walls in the distance.

The final few miles entering Rome would have been
spectacular. Huge monumental tombs lined both sides of the
road. Roman law forbade the burial of the dead within the city
walls. The poor were buried underground (hence the

Catacombs). The rich purchased plots of land outside the walls along certain main arteries and constructed huge family mausoleums. To this day the remains of many of these tombs can be seen on the Appian Way. Today what is left is the red brick substructure of the buildings which were once faced with sparkling white marble. Ancient Roman families sought to outdo each other with embellishments and statues. The architectural beauty must have been astounding.

A few hundred meters further and Paul would have entered Rome at the Servian wall, built to protect Rome in 375 BC. A large section of the Servian wall can be seen outside of Stazione Termini, Rome's main rail station. Only a small part of the original gate remains on the Appian Way, just before where the Circus Maximus now stands. Through this ancient portal (Portal Capena) Paul set foot in Rome. But this destination meant imprisonment, and conflict with a powerful and ruthless leader.

Nero

Nero's mother, Agrippina, was a scheming murderess. She willingly committed incest with her uncle, had him murdered, and placed her son upon the throne. Nero came to power when he was just seventeen years old. In comparison to his predecessors, the handsome youth was an able ruler. His government forbade contests in the circus involving bloodshed, banned capital punishment, reduced taxes, and accorded permission to slaves to bring civil complaints against unjust masters. But he had a restless spirit. In a bloody thirty-five month period between the years 59 AD and 62 AD, he killed his mother Agrippina and his wife Octavia.

Following this furious rampage, Paul was brought before Nero. Bible scholars assume that Paul's first trial is not recorded in the book of Acts because Luke died before it took place. Most scholars agree that Paul's words in 2 Timothy 4:16-17 refer to this episode:

> "At my first defense no one came to stand by me, but all deserted me....But the Lord stood by me and strengthened me, so that through me the message might be fully proclaimed and all the Gentiles might hear it. So I was rescued from the lion's mouth."

Paul initially escaped "the lion." Why? Without a doubt Nero and those close to him knew Paul was not just a common criminal. Perhaps, Nero's conclusion matched Paul's other judges, who said, "there was no charge against him that deserved death or imprisonment" (Acts 23:29).

Two years later, ten of the fourteen regions of Rome were either destroyed or severely damaged in a fire. The Roman populace held Nero responsible for burning Rome, so Nero blamed the Christians and began a brief period of deadly persecution.

Nero's Golden Palace

Nero used the tragedy to level vast areas of Rome and build **Domus Aurea**, his golden house. It was complete with all that materialism could provide: gold, gems, beautiful shells, and a banquet hall with an ivory ceiling. But it also is one of the most significant sites in Rome for evangelical Christians because here is where the Apostle Paul likely stood trial before Nero.

Enter the garden area between gate-posts each topped with a cement bust of Nero. Continue up the hill 100 yards and on your left a large path leads to the entrance of the palace. This massive complex was constructed in three short years (64-68 AD). Although it was never completed, the palace was of such magnitude Pliny states: "…Domus Aurea embraced the whole of Rome…twice we have seen the houses of the princes, Gaius and Nero, extend so far that they surround the city." Seutonius wrote: "Rome is now a single house…"[1]

The face of the palace extended more than 1,100 feet. It faced a huge artificial lake built by Nero where the Coliseum would later be erected. Inside, many of the rooms were decorated with

---

[1]Elisabetta Segla, *Domus Aurea*, p. 10, (1999: Soprintendenza Archeoligica di Roma.)

gold leaf and precious gems, covering both walls and ceiling. Vast gardens and fountains embellished the palace. Exotic birds and animals wandered everywhere. When he occupied his *"Domus"* Nero is reported by Seutonius to have exclaimed that finally he could begin to live in a house worthy of a human being."[2] In front, Nero placed a twelve story bronze statue of himself in the nude. His crown consisted of seven rays, each eighteen feet in length. This statue became known as the "Colossus" and gave the Coliseum its name.

The **golden throne room** is the suspected location where the little Jewish preacher stood testified before Nero about righteousness, resurrection, and the judgment to come. But Paul wouldn't escape and he knew it. He wrote,

> "For I am already being poured out like a drink offering, and the time has come for my departure. I have fought the good fight, I have finished the race, I have kept the faith. Henceforth there is laid up for me the crown of righteousness, which the Lord, the righteous judge, will award to me on that Day...The Lord will rescue me from every evil attack and will bring me safely to his heavenly kingdom. To him be glory for ever and ever. Amen." (2 Timothy 4:6-8, 18)

---

[2] Ibid., p. 10.

Within months of putting Paul to death, Nero was a wild, delusionary maniac. The Roman populace turned upon him in hatred. The Roman Senate condemned him to death. He fled from the Domus Aurea taking the Via Nomentana as an escape route. As the people were about to capture him, a few miles from his golden palace, he committed suicide at the youthful age of 30.

After Nero's death in 68 AD the palace was literally swept away by the emperors who followed. Nero was so hated that his palace was buried by fifteen feet of earth. First, every room was filled. Then, a hole was made in the ceiling of each room (still seen today) so slaves could pack dirt to the very top. The purpose was to erase this hated palace for all time. Instead, it was preserved for posterity in better condition than most other buildings of ancient Rome.

Lost to history for centuries, the palace was covered. Vaspasian, Titus, Domitian, Trajan and others built palaces and baths over the buried *Domus Aurea*. During the Middle Ages gardens and vineyards overtook it. Towards the end of the fifteenth century Tuscan and Umbrian artists rediscovered the palace. Raphael and other painters reproduced motifs from the *Domus Aurea* in the Vatican's *Logge*.

Today **beautiful frescos** still decorate the walls of various rooms. Many of the rooms and corridors are very large. Hundreds of slaves hustled throughout these corridors to serve Nero. The **Octagonal room** with domed ceiling was Nero's dining room. Traces can still be seen of the channels of a large waterfall that cascaded into the room. Suetonius described this dining hall as rotating continuously day and night. If it did, nothing remains today that would show how it was made to rotate.

The Coliseum

"While stands the Coliseum, Rome shall stand;
When falls the Coliseum, Rome shall fall;
And when Rome falls -- the world."
Lord Byron, Childe Harold's Pilgrimage

This greatest and most magnificent of ancient Rome's amphitheaters was constructed a few years after the Apostle Paul's death in Rome. Begun by Vespasian around 72 AD, it was completed within eight years and inaugurated by his son Titus in 80 AD. Well engineered, the entire stadium could be covered with a series of canvas sails, if needed, to protect people from the hot sun or cover them in the rain.

The Coliseum was the scene of some of the bloodiest gladiator battles known to history. Gladiators fought for their lives before cheering crowds. The ruins show the remains of rooms underneath the wooden floor that once housed animal cages and other mechanics necessary for producing the games. Sometimes, the floor was covered with canvas and flooded with water to a depth of three or four feet for the gladiator "Navel battles".

The Gladiators entered through what was known as the "Gate of death" located at the far southeast end of the stadium. Here they met crowds of up to 50,000 people. Spectators were seated in several distinct levels according to their social class (nobility, freemen, etc). If you face the floor toward the southeast, (Constantine's Arch outside will be to your right), you can clearly see the remains of the Emperor's box seat in the middle of the amphitheater. From here he witnessed the bloody spectacles with his family and friends. From here the Emperor gave his thumbs up or thumbs down sign that sentenced a fallen Gladiator to life or death. Rome's most famous Gladiator "stars" won greater fame, and sometimes freedom, if they survived. Those who lived exited the Coliseum through the "Gate of Life" (now the present day entrance).

Circus Maximus

Historical records do not prove that Christians were actually martyred in the Coliseum. But only one kilometer away is an oval basin, nearly 600 meters long, where thousands were killed. The Circus Maximus originally seated 150,000 people in wooden bleachers to watch a race track and later Gladiator games. During the reign of Constantine, the Circus could hold between 200,000 and 250,000 people. Though now a public garden, the soil is bathed in the blood of martyrs. We know that in this arena Christians were used to entertain the bloodthirsty fans of Rome. This thirst for brutal entertainment and base distraction, called "bread and games", was one of the reasons for Rome's decline and fall.

Basilica of San Clemente

Not far from Domus Aurea is the earliest place of Christian worship unearthed in Rome. The present church was built in 1108. Below it are the remains of a Roman house belonging to Titus Flavius Clemens, Roman Consul and cousin of the Emperor Domitian (81-96 AD) Their home contained a first-century pagan chapel used to worship the mystery cult, Mithra, but after Titus and his wife converted to Christianity they turned their chapel into a secret "house church". This place is one of the earliest Christian worship centers found in Rome. In the fourth century the chapel was enlarged into an actual Church building. Three ancient levels of the church and house may be visited.

When you leave the Basilica, walk back towards the Coliseum and on your way you will pass the ruins of the gladiators' dormitories. **Ludus Magnus** housed gladiators who were scheduled to fight in the nearby Coliseum and also provided a small training arena for them to prepare for battle.

Arch of Constantine

The first Christian Emperor of Rome was Constantine. He is
thought to have been born February 27, 280 AD and was
brought up in the courts of Diocletian located in what is now
modern Turkey. His father was an Army officer raised to the
rank of Caesar in 293 AD. His mother was Helena, who was
divorced by her husband in 289 AD. Although historians blame
Constantine (not unjustly) for the secularization of Christianity
because he "force converted" his troops without gaining their
personal commitment to Christ, few give due credit to the reality
of his Christian faith.

Constantine encountered Christianity during the 10th and final
persecution of Christians under Diocletian's reign and made a
personal and profound commitment to the Christian God, Jesus
Christ. His battle for the throne was motivated by a vision of the
Cross of Christ high in the sky. He heard a heavenly voice say,
"By this sign, you shall conquer." Constantine ordered a cross to
be painted on the shields of all his soldiers. The magnificent
Arch of Constantine erected in 312 AD on the northwest side
of the Coliseum, was built to praise God for aiding his victory
over his brother-in-law, Maxentius, who contended for the
throne. Constantine attributed his success and position to Christ.

After consolidating his power in 312 AD, Constantine went
to the northern city of Mediolanum (modern Milan). There he
concluded a pact with Licinius, Emperor of the Western half of

the Empire. The pact, known as the *Edict of Milan*, extended toleration to all Christians and restored any personal and corporate property that had been confiscated during the persecution of Diocletian. In 324 AD Constantine defeated Licinius and became the sole ruler of both East and West. He had Licinius executed in 325 AD

Also in 325 AD, Constantine called the Council of Nicaea to resolve and combat the Arian heresy. Arius declared that Jesus was a created being and not divine. His heresy was spreading from his church in Alexandria, Egypt, where he was a pastor, to many other Christian communities. Constantine's personal commitment to Christ spurred him to call church leaders together to resolve this threat to orthodox Christianity. This first church council (after the Jerusalem Council which is reported in Acts 15) condemned Arianism and produced the Nicene Creed. The Creed declared that Jesus was of one and the same substance as God and as Son he had absolute equality with the Father.

Before you leave the Ach of Constantine, cross the street so that you can closely inspect the Bas Relief. This form of raised sculpture depicts Titus's triumphant entrance into Rome. His cortege is carrying the booty he has brought from Jerusalem. Clearly seen are the "Ark of the Covenant" and the Jewish candelabra.   This Bas Relief reveals what these objects really looked like. The Ark and the candelabra were within the Holy of

Holies when Jesus died on the cross and the curtain that shielded them from view was shredded in two from top to bottom. Tradition maintains that the Ark and the other objects were eventually thrown into the Tiber river.

The Roman Forum

Every political, religious, or financial event concerning a Roman city developed around the Forum. The Forum was the very hub of life. Events either started here or cast their reflection here. The Roman Forum being the center of Rome's civic and economic life, was located between the Capitoline and Palatine Hills, the Imperial Forums, and the Coliseum.

This monumental complex, played a prominent role in both the Republican era (509 to 27 BC) and the Imperial age (27 BC to 476 AD). The splendor of this Forum mirrored the magnificence of the Empire. The Forum displays more than the history of Rome itself. It points to the history of all Italy and of the Mediterranean world. The Forum was the umbilical cord of Rome's extension to the known world. René Seindal writes,

"The importance of the Forum area is indicated by the presence of many of the central political, religious and judicial buildings in Rome. The Regia was the residence of the kings, and later of the rex sacrorum and pontifex maximus. The Curia, was the meeting place of the Senate and the Comitium and the Rostra, where public meetings were held. Major temples and sanctuaries in the Forum include the Temple of Castor and Pollux, the Temple of Saturn and the Temple of Vesta. Commercial and judicial activities took place in the basilicas, the two remaining are the Basilica Aemilia and the Basilica Julia."[3]

In this Forum Julius Caesar and Caesar Augustus presided over Rome's Senators. Here, Mark Anthony gave Caesar's eulogy so aptly depicted by Shakespeare's "Friends, Romans, and Countrymen, lend me your ears!" Roman commoners came here to worship in the temples. Religious processions solemnly walked through the Forum and up the Capitoline Hill to the Temple of Jupiter, where they sacrificed bulls to celebrate military victories. At the Temple of Vesta, an eternal flame burned for this Roman goddess of hearth and fire. Romans believed this sacred fire was closely tied to the fortunes of the city and viewed its extinction as

[3] http://sights.seindal.dk/sight/4_Forum_Romanum.html

SEEING ROME & CHRISTIAN ITALY

an omen of disaster. In the Temple of Saturn, worshippers prayed to the ancient Roman god of fertility for a good harvest.

But amidst all this pagan worship, faithful Christians also walked these very streets to share the good news of Jesus Christ.

Via Sacra, the main street of the Forum, had become the gathering place for crowds. It is easy to envision Paul preaching to these crowds after his release from his first imprisonment. As people were milling about amongst the splendors of this glistening Forum, could it be that Paul fulfilled his longing,

"To preach the gospel to you also who are in Rome."[4]

Arch of Titus

Located within the Forum is the Arch of Titus. Emperor Titus, as with every other Roman emperor, thought himself to be god. The inscription at the top of the Arch says,

"The Roman Senate and People to Deified Titus, Vespasian Augustus, son of Deified Vespasian."

This monument was erected by Titus in 81 AD after he led his Roman army to attack and destroy Jerusalem in 70 AD. This arch was built to commemorate his victory over the Jews.

---

[4] Romans 1:15

However, what Titus did not know was that his victory fulfilled Jesus' prophecy from forty years earlier. Matthew 24:1-2 says,

> Jesus left the temple and was going away, when his
> disciples came to point out to him the buildings of
> the temple. But he answered them, "You see all
> these, do you not? Truly, I say to you, there will not
> be left here one stone upon another that will not be
> thrown down."

Jesus' prediction was so important that it was recorded in all four Gospels. Now, the Arch of Titus is proof for everyone to see that Jesus was right.

Mamertine Prison

At the foot of the Roman Forum, down the stone stairs, you find the oldest, most historic prison in Rome. Now known as St. Peter's prison, tradition has long favored this as the place where the Apostle Paul was jailed for his final imprisonment.

In Paul's day prisoners were lowered into the prison area through a hole that still exists in the ceiling of the prison (it's now covered with a grate). Some were strangled or decapitated. Their bodies were often thrown into a tributary of the Tiber River and carried out to sea by the river's flow. (The large iron door in the prison itself opens to stairs leading to the tributary.) If this is where Paul's final cell held him, then this is where he sat in near darkness, with only a small oil lamp for light and no coat to ward off the cold of winter to write his final words.

Once you are in the prison and have seen the ancient frescoes of Jesus and Peter, put down your audio guide, skip the rest of tour, and instead read the words of the Apostle Paul's final letter to his co-laborer, Timothy and picture what it would have been like for him:

> Always be sober-minded, endure suffering, do the work of an evangelist, fulfill your ministry. For I am already being poured out as a drink offering, and the time of my departure has come. I have fought the good fight, I have finished the race, I have kept the faith. Henceforth there is laid up for me the crown of righteousness, which the Lord, the righteous judge, will award to me on that Day, and not only to me but also to all who have loved his appearing. Do your best to come to me soon...When you come, bring the cloak that I left with Carpus at Troas, also the books, and above all the parchments....Do your best to come before winter.
>
> (2 Timothy 4:5-9, 13, 21)

Many other famous convicts awaited trial before Caesar in this underground cave. Among them was Lucius Aelius Sejanus, head of the Pretorian Guard in 31 AD. Sejanus was thought to be plotting the death of Caesar Tiberius so he could become Emperor. Meanwhile, Pontus Pilate, the Governor Sejanus had appointed over Palestine, was nervous of being associated with his friend's plot. Pilate had a complicated judicial decision to make. He was convinced that a preacher from Nazareth was not guilty, but he feared the consequences if any accusation of disloyalty to Caesar Tiberius was made.

> From then on Pilate sought to release him, but the Jews cried out, "If you release this man, you are not Caesar's friend. Everyone who makes himself a king opposes Caesar." So when Pilate heard these words, he brought Jesus out and sat down on the judgment seat at a place called The Stone Pavement, and in Aramaic Gabbatha. Now it was the day of Preparation of the Passover. It was about the sixth hour. He said to the Jews, "Behold your King!" They cried out, "Away with him, away with him, crucify him!" Pilate said to them, "Shall I crucify your King?" The chief priests answered, "We have no king but Caesar." So he delivered him over to them to be crucified.   (John 19:12-16)

The Vatican
&
St. Peter's Basilica

As you cross the white marble boundary line, you leave the country of Italy and enter the world's smallest nation, the Vatican City State. It is only 500 meters square, but adds to its Vatican city boundary also the three basilicas (St. Mary Major, St. John Lateran, and St. Paul Outside the Gate), the Pontifical palace located in Castel Gandolfo, and the Cancelleria Palace. It has a fixed population of 282 residents plus 110 Swiss guards.

The **Vatican Museum** is one of the greatest museums of the world, a must-see for all who come to Rome. The famous **Sistine Chapel** was constructed in 1475-1481 on the order of Pope Sixtus IV. This chapel was decorated with what many authorities conclude are the greatest works of art produced during the Renaissance. The magnificence of Botticelli,

Signorelli, Piero di Cosimo, Perugino, Michaelangelo and Raphael produced masterpieces that overwhelm with grandeur.

Also, worthy of being seen are the ancient **Bible manuscripts** (*Vaticanus, etc.*), a **statue of Caesar Augustus** at age of 40, the **Laoconte statue** found in Nero's Domus Aurea, **the Raphael rooms**, and **the relics** once kept in the Sancta Santorum when Martin Luther made his pilgrimage to the top of the Scala Sancta in hopes of freeing himself of his sinful guilt.

St. Peter's Basilica

The original basilica was begun under Emperor Constantine in 320 AD. Pope Nicolas V began retrofitting the old church in 1452, but Pope Julius II (1503-1513) went much farther. He decided to replace the old basilica with the majesty and grandeur of the present. This work continued for one hundred eleven years until completed in 1614 and consecrated on the basilica's 1300th anniversary, November 18, 1626.

The immensity of this church is difficult to conceive. It covers a surface of five and half acres and rises 446 feet from the base to the top of the cross on the dome (*cupola*) designed by Michelangelo.   The **double colonnades** (284 columns in all) surrounding the square were designed by Bernini in the form of two arms meant to symbolize that the arms of the church are open to the world. The **thirteen statues** above the facade are those of Jesus, John the Baptist and all the apostles except Peter.

The **central balcony** above the entrance of the basilica is where the election of a new Pope is announced to the Roman public and the world. The **Papal apartment** can be seen from the square facing the basilica. It is the next to top story of the building on the right. The three windows on the far right are those of the Pope's residence. He often blesses the crowds on Sunday mornings from the middle window. Before entering the church, note the cemented **Holy Doors**. These doors were opened once every 50 years for Jubilee year, but now Jubilee is held every 25 years.

Inside the basilica, **La Pietà** is considered one of Michelangelo's greatest works. It has been placed behind glass since a deranged man threw acid on it in 1972. To the left, facing the Pietà, is the **tomb of Christina of Sweden**. She was the first Lutheran royalty to be re-converted to Catholicism. At her conversion it was declared: "The tide has turned, Scandinavia will return to the Mother Church." Christina's body was interred in St. Peter's as testimony that Scandinavia would be reconverted.

Beneath the **Papal Altar** is the alleged burial place of the Apostle Peter. Also, on the right there is a bronze statue of Peter and notice how the toes have been worn away by the adoring kisses and touches by faithful pilgrims visiting the Basilica.

Bernini's Tomb of Pope Alexander VII (1655-67) depicts Justice seated with her foot on the world globe precisely over

England. Justice specifically stamps England under foot because it embraced the Anglican church.

The story is told that one of the Catholic Church's great theologians was showing a friend the beauties of St. Peter's. As they stood before the stone mosaic of Peter, John and the lame beggar he commented: "The church no longer is able to say 'Silver and gold have we none,' but it is also not able to say 'Rise, take up thy bed and walk.'"

So many important historical events have taken place in St. Peter's that it is impossible to name them all. Noteworthy is the Coronation of Charlemagne on Christmas night 800 AD. He knelt and received the Imperial crown of the Holy Roman Empire from Pope Leo III.

The world's largest church, though not Protestant, is directly connected to the rise of the Protestant Reformation. St. Peter's could not have been accomplished without a massive infusion of finances. Unfortunately from the Middle Ages Christian generosity rarely met the needs of the church. So the clergy resorted to their own means: teaching the existence of Purgatory and the value of prayers and indulgences in freeing the souls of those incarcerated therein. They taught that these prayers and indulgences could be purchased from the church and its clergy. Fund-raisers were commissioned by the Popes to sell indulgences. When Johann Tetzel arrived in Wittenberg, Germany, hawking these indulgences, his appeals enraged Martin

Luther. Tetzel famously said, "At the sound of the in coin in the plate, another soul flies out of Purgatory." It was not long before the Protestant Reformers revved into high gear.

St. John Lateran's Basilica

This basilica is still described as "Mother and chief of all the churches of Rome and of the World." Built by Constantine in 313-318 AD, the original basilica was similar to the first basilica of St. Peter. It has been remodeled many times, but maintains its original ceiling and floor from the fifth century. The imposing façade was added in 1732-1735. Inside the colossal statues of the apostles were added before 1718.

The baptistery was built by Constantine at the same time as the church. Christian baptism was originally only by immersion, hence the pool-type construction. The exterior was remodeled in 1637 by Urban VIII.

In front of St. John Lateran's is the oldest and tallest obelisk in Rome, the **Obelisk of Thutmose III**. Originally from ancient Egypt and dated to the fifteenth century BC, it is likely that Moses would have seen this obelisk. In 357 AD Constantine brought it to Rome from Ammon in Thebes and placed in the

Circus Maximus. It fell and disappeared beneath the ruins, until its re-discovery in 1586. It was then erected outside the Lateran Palace by Sixtus V.

The **Lateran Palace**, from the fourth century BC, was built over property that had long belonged to the Emperors. Nero confiscated this property from the Lateran family after it had participated in the Congiura of the Pisoni (65 AD). It was used as the headquarters for Septimius Severus' imperial cavalry (197 AD) and was donated by Constantine to the Church of Rome. The bishops of Rome resided here until 1377. In 1585-90 Sixtus V destroyed the original Palace, retaining only the Scala Sancta, the Chapel of San Lorenzo in Palatio (the so-called Sancta Sanctorum, now at the top of the stairs, and the remains of the triclinium of Leo III. In 1929 the Roman Church signed a Concordat with Mussolini and the Lateran buildings became a part of the Vatican State along with the other two basilicas.

Nearby, you'll find the famous **Scala Sancta**. According to tradition, these are the steps to Pontius Pilate's palace upon which Jesus tread as he was taken to Pilate for judgment. Constantine's mother Helen brought them from Jerusalem to Rome. Drops of the Savior's blood are said to be found on some of the stairs (which are now protected by wooden stairs with glass over the spots of blood).

Pilgrims mount the 28 stairs on their knees, pausing on each stair to say the Rosary. An indulgence of ten years off purgatory is granted for each step. Martin Luther joined other pilgrims in climbing the stairs of the Scala Sancta on his own pilgrimage to Rome. He hoped to assuage the guilt of sin, but upon his return to Germany, he noted in his journal that not even mounting the stairs of the Scala Sancta diminished his guilt. It was after this that he concluded: "The just shall live by faith alone."

At the head of the stairs is the Sancta Santorum (the Chapel of San Lorenzo in Palatio, the private chapel of the popes) which during the Middle Ages contained Christendom's greatest and best relics. The acheropita, image of Jesus not made by human hand, was laminated in silver by Innocence III (1198-1216). This image is supposed to be a true representation of what Jesus' looked like. Additionally, they claim a vial of Mary's milk, the foreskin of Jesus from his circumcision when he was days old, and many others.

Tradition says **the Basilica of Santa Croce in Gerusalemme** was first a chapel inside the villa of Helen, the mother of Constantine. Once Christianity was declared legal, she built a small church to preserve relics of the cross and earth from beneath the cross that she brought from Jerusalem. In 1144 Lucio II reconstructed it in the form of a basilica. Its present form was remodeled in 1743. The earth and original relics are said to be under the pavement of the Chapel of Helen accessible by the stairs descending from the right side of the *Abside*.

Despite the fact there is no evidence of their historicity, many travelers visit the Chapel of the Relics to see the alleged three fragments of the Cross, a nail that pierced Jesus' body, part of the sign INRI placed over the Savior's head, two thorns from the crown of thorns, a piece of the sponge offered to Jesus while on the cross, one of the pieces of silver given to Judas, the finger of the Apostle Thomas that touched Jesus' wounds, and the entire crossbar from the cross of the good thief.

Porta Maggiore is a majestic arch built by Caligola (38-52 AD) and finished by Emperor Claudio. It supported two major aqueducts that supplied water to Rome. It was incorporated within the Aurelian walls as a gate between 270-275 AD. The inscription repeats the names of Claudius, Vespasian, and Titus on both sides of the façade. The latter two restored the arch in 71 and 81 AD.

A little less than two kilometers northwest is **Santa Maria Maggiore**, the mother church of all St. Mary churches in the world. The bell tower (75 meters) is Rome's tallest and was built in 1377. The façade was added in the middle of the eighteenth century. Despite the many modifications, the inside of the church has retained its original appearance. The mosaics from the fifth century reproduce scenes from the Old Testament. In the *confessional* of the church is a reliquary containing the crib from Bethlehem in which the baby Jesus lay.

Ostia Antica

Few tourists realize that less than fifteen miles from Rome, on the shores of the Mediterranean Sea, the splendid remains of an entire ancient city may be visited. It was here that Monica, mother of St. Augustine died in 387 AD.

Lacking only the vivid frescoes of Pompei, Ancient Ostia is in many ways as spectacular as Pompeii. Three stories of what were once five story buildings remain in place. The original marble staircases are open and available to be climbed by visitors. The conduits of the water system are on view. The original streets are uncovered. The bathhouses, stores and pubs are readily recognizable. This port city and ancient gateway to Rome was founded in the fourth century BC by Anco Marzio, the fourth King of Rome. Originally the city was a waterfront city, but centuries of silt, from the nearby Tiber River, has removed the shores of the sea to several miles away.

Mosaics adorn the various bathhouses of the city, especially those of the Terme of Nettuno (Neptune). Ostia's mosaics are noted for their black and white patterns.

Enjoy climbing stairs to second and third floors that are well worn by centuries of use by Ostians of long ago. The public toilets in Via della Forica on the east side of the Forum will provide a moment of laughter. Don't miss them.

The commercial life of a Roman city may be seen in Ostia better than in Pompei. The Piazzale delle Corporazioni is the only one of its kind to be seen in Italy. This is a vast open area measuring 107 by 78 meters. It opens toward a temple dedicated to the god Vulcan. Around the square were 70 rooms used by the import merchants. Grain was the major merchandise that passed through this port. Following the main street, Via Massimo to where it takes a diagonal left turn and becomes Via Decumano, past the Basilica Giudiziaria (Hall of Justice) on the left, across from the Tempio Rotondo on the right, visit the Christian Church (Basilica). This church is a testimony to the expansion of the Gospel in the entire Rome area. It was not built, however, until Constantine made Christianity legal throughout the empire.

The Castle of Julius II

Erected on the banks of the Tiber River, which once flowed through this area, Martin V (1417-1431) erected the tower as an advanced post of defense for Rome. While he was still Cardinal, Julian della Rovere, the future Pope Julius II, built the castle portion. This is another example of Della Rovere's fondness for construction projects that became an effective cause of the Protestant Reformation when he became Pope.

Central Italy

Florence

Florence is the jewel of the Mediterranean, if not the world. In 2007 it was voted as the most desirable destination for tourists. Home to Dante, Petrarch, Macchiavelli, Michelangelo, Leonardo Da Vinci, Alberti, Boticelli and Brunelleschi, Florence gave birth to the Renaissance and now attracts millions of tourists each year.

Florence (*Firenze*) was founded in 59 BC as a Roman colony by Julius Caesar. It became the richest and most influential city in the Middle Ages. But to see Florence as Christian, is not to follow the biblical history as we have done other places, but to pay attention to the art history that portrayed biblical scenes.

The Duomo

Begin your tour of Florence in **Piazza di San Giovanni**, the true heart of the city. There you'll find the third largest church after St. Peter's in Rome and St. Paul's in London. Commonly called the **Duomo**, construction began on this Basilica di Santa Maria del Fiore in 1296 and finished in 1468. It is especially noteworthy for the huge octagonal cupola done by Filippo Brunelleschi.

Also, in this piazza is one of the oldest religious edifices of Florence, **The Baptistry of St. John**. Built between the 12th and 13th centuries, it is where Florence's most famous citizens were baptized. Dante, in his renowned *Divine Comedy*, mentions this baptistry as "the fount of my baptism". The doors of the baptistry are worthy of special note.

The **south door** is the most ancient, built by Andrea Pisano in 1330. At the top are twenty scenes from the Life of John the Baptist, who was considered the protector saint of Florence. The bottom eight scenes depict humility and the cardinal virtues.

The **north door** was the first door made by Lorenzo Ghiberti (from 1403-1424). The top 20 scenes depict various New Testament events and the bottom eight show the four Evangelists (Matthew, Mark, Luke and John) and four Church Fathers.

The **east door** is a reproduction of Ghiberti's famous "Porta del Paradiso" (Gates to Paradise). Arthur Lubow in the November 2007 Smithsonian Magazine comments that "These panels are one of the defining masterpieces of the Italian Renaissance."

The seventeenth church council met here in January 1439, in

order to reunify the Roman church with the Greek Orthodox church. Although an agreement was reached and signed by Greek Orthodox Patriarch Joseph II of Constantinople, the Eastern Church refused to accept the agreement and remains to this day a separate denomination from Rome.

David

The foremost work of art in the city of Florence is of a prominent biblical character, David. Three famous David statues are located in Florence. Donatello's life-sized nude represents a youthful David standing triumphantly over Goliath's head. Andrea del Verrocchio's David is cast in bronze. But Michelangelo's David, found in the **Galleria dell' Accademia,** is the most famous of the three. Sculptured between 1502 and 1504, this seventeen foot masterpiece was carved from one gigantic block of marble.

Not far from the Accademia is the **Museo di San Marco**. This church and convent were home to a well-known Renaissance preacher named Girolamo Savonarola. Born in Ferrara, he entered religious life as a monk in the city of Bologna. At the age of twenty-nine he was transferred to Florence by his Father Superior.

During this time the ruler of the Florentine republic, Lorenzo de' Medici, died and was seceded by his son Piero. But after two years the populace drove him out of office and into exile. In this political vacuum Savonarola became the effective leader of the city. So popular was his preaching that he was invited to preach from the pulpit of the Duomo. His fiery and reforming sermons, which attacked the sin, corruption, and immorality of Florence's populace, were used by God to transform the hearts of thousands of Florentines.

Near the famous **Ponte Vecchio** bridge is the **Piazza della Signoria**. This square, surrounded by Gelato shops and tables with umbrellas now invites relaxation, but long ago it was filled with hundreds who had come to see the hanging and burning of Girolamo Savonarola and his two fellow monks. Savonarola was forced to watch the torture, hanging and burning of each of his closest co-workers. The crowd, made up of *The Arrabbiati* (The Angry Ones), hurled curses and insults at him as he was tortured and hung. A few Florentine citizens, who had given their hearts to Christ as a result of Savonarola's powerful preaching, watched in silence. When his time came, he peacefully submitted to inhuman torture and was then hanged. Savonarola's body was burned and his ashes were thrown into the Arno River.

Assisi

This city is not famous in and of itself; rather it is remembered because of one of its sons, Giovanni Bernadone (St. Francis of Assisi-1182-1226). How Giovanni Battista became known as Francis is not known. His father traded cloth from France and his mother was French. Some believe this to be the source of his name change.

Assisi's vigorous commerce kept it in perennial conflict with its larger neighbor, Perugia, twenty-six kilometers across the valley. The two-hilltop cities fought over the rich farmland below them and control of the region. During the war of 1202 Assisi was defeated and twenty-year old Giovanni (Francis) was taken captive. He spent a year in a Perugia prison.

Later, Francis set out on a campaign against Perugia in command of a brigade of soldiers. The night before the conflict he had dream. A voice told him to turn back. He obeyed the voice and upon returning home experienced a radical conversion to Christ. Upon his conversion Francis dedicated himself to poverty, chastity and obedience. Francis gathered twelve followers, who along with him, dedicated themselves to imitate the life of Christ. The three principles of their commitment were known as *Regula Prima*. In 1210 the *Regula Prima* received approval by Pope Innocent III and the Franciscans became an official order of the Roman church. There is no doubt that this young man's faith in Christ was real. He became a passionate evangelist that nearly brought Italy its first nationwide revival.

The saint is buried in the Basilica that bears his name. The two-tiered church is renowned for its frescoes done by Giotto, Cimabue and other Italian masters.

Clare of Assisi (1194-1253) was also born into a wealthy Assisi family. Heavily influenced by Francis, she abandoned her family's wealth and ran away from home to live in a monastery. With Francis she co-founded the order of the Poor Clares. She is buried in the basilica in the valley below Assisi.

A Prayer for Italy

Italy has never experienced the renewing spiritual power that the Welch revival brought to Wales or Whitefield, Moody and Billy Sunday brought to America. In Italy there are so many who have not seen the beauty and glory of Jesus Christ. Please pray for God's continued work in Italy. Below are four prayers to help you begin:

- Father in Heaven, I pray that you'd bring about revival in Italy during my lifetime. May you remove the barriers to a true understanding of the gospel so that millions would turn to you.

- Father, I pray that you would send more laborers into your Italian harvest. Please call many missionaries who have spiritual stamina, emotional maturity, cultural adaptability and great faith.

- Father, please birth several church-planting movements of healthy, Bible-based churches. Please strengthen your work in Rome, Milan, and Florence so that it radiates out to the rest of the country.

- Father, I ask you to strengthen the Bible schools and seminaries. Help them to adequately train their students in sound doctrine and prepare them for ministry. Please bless them with an increase in student numbers, godly and gifted professors, and sufficient resources.

In Jesus' Name,

Amen

Made in the USA
Monee, IL
13 February 2023